Honest to
Goodness

Honest to Goodness

WILLIAM LUOMA

**Sermons for the
Sundays After Pentecost
(Sundays in Ordinary Time)
MIDDLE THIRD**

CYCLE C FIRST LESSON TEXTS FROM THE COMMON LECTIONARY

C.S.S. Publishing Co., Inc.
Lima, Ohio

HONEST TO GOODNESS

Copyright © 1988 by
The C.S.S. Publishing Company, Inc.
Lima, Ohio

All rights reserved. No part of this publication may be reproduced, stored in a retrieval system, or transmitted in any form or by any means, electronic, mechanical, photocopying, recording, or otherwise, without the prior permission of the publisher. Inquiries should be addressed to: The C.S.S. Publishing Company, Inc., 628 South Main Street, Lima, Ohio 45804.

Library of Congress Cataloging-in-Publication Data

Luoma, William, 1934-
    Honest to goodness: sermons for the Sundays after Pentecost (Sundays in ordinary time) middle third / William Luoma.
        p.   cm.
    Includes bibliographical references.
    ISBN 1-556-73061-6
    1. Church year sermons 2. Bible. O.T.—Sermons. I. Title.
BV4253.L86   1988
252'.6—dc19
                                                    88-3191
                                                      CIP

8858 / ISBN 1-55673-061-6   PRINTED IN U.S.A.

Table of Contents

A Note Concerning Lectionaries and Calendars 7

A Personal Word 9

Proper 11[1] Pentecost 9[2] Ordinary Time 16[3]	*I Kid You Not* *2 Kings 4:8-17*	10
Proper 12 Pentecost 10 Ordinary Time 17	*The Preposterous Prescription* *2 Kings 5:1-15ab*	17
Proper 13 Pentecost 11 Ordinary Time 18	*Do Not Go Gentle* *Into that Good Night* *2 Kings 13:14-20a*	26
Proper 14 Pentecost 12 Ordinary Time 19 (RC)	*The Focus on Fitness* *Jeremiah 18:1-11*	33
Proper 15 Pentecost 13 Ordinary Time 20	*I Never Promised You* *a Rose Garden* *Jeremiah 20:7-13*	40
Proper 16 Pentecost 14 Ordinary Time 21	*The Cracked Crystal Ball* *Jeremiah 28:1-9*	48
Proper 17 Pentecost 15 Ordinary Time 22	*. . . and Justice for All* *Ezekiel 18:1-9, 25-29*	55

Proper 18
Pentecost 16
Ordinary Time 23

Why I Can't Sleep in Church 62
Ezekiel 33:1-11

Proper 19
Pentecost 17
Ordinary Time 24

Honest-to-Goodness Religion 69
Hosea 4:1-3; 5:15—6:6

Proper 20
Pentecost 18
Ordinary Time 25

The God Who Doesn't Give Up 77
Hosea 11:1-11

Common Lectionary
Lutheran Lectionary
Roman Catholic Lectionary

A Note Concerning Lectionaries and Calendars

The following index will aid the user of this book in matching the right Sunday with the appropriate text during the second half of the church year. Days listed here include only those appropriate to the contents of this book.

Fixed-date Lectionaries

Common	Roman Catholic	Lutheran Lectionary
Proper 11	Ordinary Time 16 *July 17-23*	Pentecost 9
Proper 12	Ordinary Time 17 *July 24-30*	Pentecost 10
Proper 13	Ordinary Time 18 *July 31 — August 6*	Pentecost 11
Proper 14	Ordinary Time 19 *August 7-13*	Pentecost 12
Proper 15	Ordinary Time 20 *August 14-20*	Pentecost 13
Proper 16	Ordinary Time 21 *August 21-27*	Pentecost 14
Proper 17	Ordinary Time 22 *August 28 — September 3*	Pentecost 15

Common	Roman Catholic	Lutheran Lectionary
Proper 18 *September 4-10*	Ordinary Time 23	Pentecost 16
Proper 19 *September 11-17*	Ordinary Time 24	Pentecost 17
Proper 20 *September 18-24*	Ordinary Time 25	Pentecost 18

A Personal Word

"Honest to goodness!" Now there's an innocent-sounding phrase. "Honest to goodness" describes the flavor of a freshly-brewed cup of coffee, or the aroma of down-home cooking, or a loaf of homemade bread just out of the oven. "Honest to goodness" is something that is real, genuine, and authentic.

In this series of Old Testament texts, some of which are baffling, and some of which are quite clear, one prophetic call stands out. That is the call for God's people to be authentic, real and genuine. The prophets have no tolerance for pretenders, or fakes, or those with a long list of excuses. There is no mistaking the call for God's people to be sincere and faithful, with an "honest to goodness" flavor.

Bill Luoma

One day Elisha went on to Shunem, where a wealthy woman lived, who urged him to eat some food. So whenever he passed that way, he would turn in there to eat food. And she said to her husband, "Behold now, I perceive that this is a holy man of god, who is continually passing our way. Let us make a small roof chamber with walls, and put there for him a bed, a table, a chair, and a lamp, so that whenever he comes to us, he can go in there."

One day he came there, and turned into the chamber and rested there. And he said to Gehazi his servant, "Call this Shunammite." When he had called her, she stood before him. And he said to him, "Say now to her, See, you have taken all this trouble for us; what is to be done for you? Would you have a word spoken on your behalf to the king or to the commander of the army?" She answered, "I dwell among my own people." And he said, "What then is to be done for her?" Gehazi answered, "Well, she has no son, and her husband is old." He said, "Call her." And when he had called her, she stood in the doorway. And he said, "At this season, when the time comes round, you shall embrace a son." And she said, "No my lord, O man of God; do not lie to your maidservant." But the woman conceived, and she bore a son about that time the following spring, as Elisha had said to her.

2 Kings 4:8-17

2 Kings 4:8-17   Proper 11 (C)
                                                Pentecost 9 (L)
                                           Ordinary Time 16 (RC)

I Kid You Not

"At this season, when the time comes round, you shall embrace a son." (v. 16)

Prayer: *Amid all the voices clamoring for our attention in this world, we thank you, O Lord, that your word is still truth. Amen.*

One of the hosts of television's "Tonight Show," preceding Johnny Carson, was the articulate host, Jack Paar. Near the height of his career, Jack Paar wrote a book titled *I Kid You Not*. This was a phrase Jack Paar often used, to convince the audience that he wasn't joking, but telling the truth. He said in his book that what has pleased him most about the success of the show is that it is a triumph of honesty. "Whenever I say something and add, 'I kid you not,' I'm not kidding! It's a modest show of light conversation and pleasant entertainment, but it's live and real and true."[1]

And what does this have to do with Second Kings? The phrase, "I kid you not," that Jack Paar made famous, is one that fits this episode between the Old Testament prophet Elisha and the wealthy woman of Shunem who furnished an original "Bed and Breakfast" for her holy guest.

This encounter is one of several events recorded in the fourth chapter of Second Kings. It is there with the amazing

---

1. Jack Paar, *I Kid You Not*, Little, Brown & Co., 1960, p. 79.

jar of oil that did not run out, and the sun-stricken boy who was brought back to life. It is there with the poisoned stew that was neutralized by the man of God, and the miraculous feeding of a hundred men with only twenty loaves of bread.

A wealthy woman of Shunem showed hospitality to Elisha the prophet as he passed by. She not only invited him to stop and eat, but arranged for a special room for him to stay. As a sign of gratitude, Elisha offered to do something for her. When she declined his offer to speak a good word on her behalf to the king, he promised her a child.

When she heard this, the childless woman said, "Whatever you do, please don't lie to me!" This was not a matter to be taken lightly. There are things you can joke about, but this was not one of them. It may be that Elisha could then have said, in a Hebrew equivalent, "I kid you not." He was saying, "I'm not kidding." You can believe this because it's God's word.

1. *God promises the Unexpected*

Here is a rich woman. She has more than most of her neighbors. When she goes to the supermarket, she doesn't have to worry whether she will have enough money to pay for the groceries in the cart. When she shops for clothes, she doesn't need to pass up a nice outfit because of the price. But there is something that she doesn't have and cannot buy. That something is a child.

When she was married, her family and her friends anticipated motherhood with her. But as the weeks and months went by, it became evident that she was not to be favored with a child. When she would go out, she would see other women with their children. When she would meet new people, the inevitable question would come up, "Do you have any children?" She had learned how to answer it politely and to hide her true feelings, but it still hurt every time it happened. She knew how her culture regarded childlessness and was keenly aware of the empty place in her life. She had reached the point of accepting her childless circumstance, and had put out of her mind any hopes of becoming a mother.

However, what this wealthy woman had accepted as certain for her life, was due to be changed. The answer came unexpectedly from the prophet she had befriended. It came from Elisha, who wanted to repay her kindness to him. He could have given her a gift, or spoken a good word for her to the king. His servant Gehazi perceived the one thing that she probably wanted and desired most. When Elisha asked, "What shall be done for her?" Gehazi answered, "Well, she has no son, and her husband is old." Elisha then promised her the birth of her own son.

For a woman who had considered herself barren, this indeed was nothing to take lightly. Here was a promise — unexpected, unsolicited, unasked for. But it was a promise which, if true, would meet one of her deepest needs and desires.

Looking back from our culture, it is somewhat difficult for us to understand this encounter between Elisha and the woman of Shunem. Elisha didn't even ask her whether she wanted a child. Isn't it rather arrogant for a man, even if he is a prophet, to prescribe a pregnancy without first consulting or asking the woman? Many women today would resent that. But this is certainly not a universal answer for every woman in every age. This is an unexpected promise given to one woman, in a particular circumstance, who evidently had a deep yearning for a child.

2. God proclaims the Unlikely

It must have seemed unlikely that the woman of Shunem would ever bear a child, yet Elisha's word to her came true. We do not know the name of her child, as we know the names of other children whose births were announced in the Scriptures, but her experience is somewhat similar to that of others.

Sarah, the wife of Abraham, was an unlikely candidate for

motherhood. When the announcement was made by three strangers that she would bear a son, she laughed because of her age. The son born to her was called Isaac, a name which means "laughter."

Rachel was the wife that Jacob loved most, but she was unhappy without children. At one point she entreated Jacob, saying "Give me children, or I shall die!" (Genesis 30:1) When she finally gave birth to Joseph, he immediately became the favorite of his father and the envy of his brothers.

First Samuel, Chapter one, is the poignant account of the woman named Hannah, who was deeply distressed because she had no children. If you read between the lines, you can sense the tension between Hannah and the other wife, Peninnah who had children. "Peninnah (her rival) used to provoke her sorely to irritate her, because the Lord had closed her womb." (1 Samuel 1:6) You can imagine Peninnah fussing with her babies in front of Hannah, feeding them and fixing clothes for them. You can imagine her day after day, rubbing it in that Hannah has no children.

Hannah went to the temple and, in her deep distress, prayed for a child. Eli the priest mistook her for a drunken woman, but she explained to him, "I have been speaking out of my great anxiety and vexation." (1 Samuel 1:16) When Hannah finally conceived and bore a son, she named him Samuel and gave him to the Lord as she had vowed.

Elizabeth, another woman advanced in years, became the mother of John the Baptizer. During her pregnancy, she said, "Thus the Lord has done to me in the days when he looked on me, to take away my reproach among men." (Luke 1:25) By speaking of her reproach, she meant her shame or disgrace. How sad. It seemed that the one and only way a woman could gain respect was to have children, and especially sons.

These women — Sarah, Rachel, Hannah and Elizabeth — appeared to be unlikely prospects for motherhood. But God intervened in their lives. He made happen what seemed unlikely to happen.

3. God programs the Unfeasible

The word "feasible" refers to something that is possible, probable, and within reason. Conversely, the word "unfeasible" is like the description a man gave about his chances of being elected to an important post at a large convention. He said he had two chances; "Slim and none." When we speak theologically, it really doesn't matter if something is unfeasible or not. God has never been hindered by what seems unfeasible.

When the angel Gabriel was telling the virgin Mary that she would be the mother of a special child, Mary said, "How can this be?" The angel spoke of the power of the Most High, and assured her "With God nothing will be impossible." (Luke 1:37) Think about that startling statement! With God, there is no "Mission Impossible."

Today, computers can be programmed to perform tasks and to make calculations which would have been impossible years ago. God, however, has always been able to program his purposes. From the days of Abraham to the birth of Christ, and to the present time, God has led and prepared his people. In our time, through his Holy Spirit, he works in and with the church. The unfeasible becomes attainable, and as the Marines say, "The impossible takes just a little longer."

One commentator sees Elisha's word as a prophetic intervention. He says:

> *It is the word or act or person of the prophet which drastically changes situations which seem hopelessly closed. The church now has no more important preaching to do than to articulate that openness because the freedom of God comes embodied in such unacceptable ways.*[2]

The church, as part of the prophetic succession, is called to

---

2. Walter Brueggemann, *2 Kings*, Knox Preaching Guides, John Knox Press, 1982, p. 18-19.

point to those things that are possible with God. But the church cannot be satisfied just to sit back and challenge others to do the work. The church needs to take God at his word and to be instrumental in changing those situations which seem hopelessly closed.

An almost unbelievable story recently appeared in the newspapers. A skydiver's nightmare turned into an amazing rescue, when Greg Robertson plunged for more than a mile, aiming for an injured woman whose parachute failed to open. He reached her just seconds before she hit the ground. The woman, Diane Williams, had been knocked out when she collided with another skydiver. Robertson, a safety instructor, pursued the woman, diving head-first, pinning his arms to his sides to reduce the wind resistance. When he caught up to her, he pulled her ripcord, and when her chute was safely open, he opened his own and both landed. The woman was hospitalized with injuries, but Robertson went back up to do some more skydiving.

Life inevitably presents us with surprises — opportunities — and blessings. Through it all, God's will continues good and trustworthy. It is the Lord God who promises the Unexpected . . . who proclaims the Unlikely . . . who programs the Unfeasible.

It is the Lord who says to you and me, "I kid you not." You can believe him because he gives you his word.

Naaman, commander of the army of the king of Syria, was a great man with his master and in high favor, because by him the Lord had given victory to Syria. He was a mighty man of valor, but he was a leper. Now the Syrians on one of their raids had carried off a little maid from the land of Israel, and she waited on Naaman's wife. She said to her mistress, "Would that my lord were with the prophet who is in Samaria! He would cure him of his leprosy." So Naaman went in and told his lord, "Thus and so spoke the maiden from the land of Israel." And the king of Syria said, "Go now, and I will send a letter to the king of Israel."

So he went, taking with him ten talents of silver, six thousand shekels of gold, and ten festal garments. And he brought the letter to the king of Israel, which read, "When this letter reaches you, know that I have sent to you Naaman my servant, that you may cure him of his leprosy." And when the king of Israel read the letter, he rent his clothes and said, "Am I God, to kill and to make alive, that this man sends words to me to cure a man of his leprosy? Only consider, and see how he is seeking a quarrel with me."

But when Elisha the man of God heard that the king of Israel had rent his clothes, he sent to the king, saying, "Why have you rent your clothes? Let him come now to me, that he may know that there is a prophet in Israel." So Naaman came with his horses and chariots, and halted at the door of Elisha's house. And Elisha sent a messenger to him saying, "Go and wash in the Jordan seven times, and your flesh shall be restored, and you shall be clean." But Naaman was angry, and went away, saying, "Behold, I thought that he would surely come out to me, and stand, and call on the name of the Lord his God, and wave his hand over the place, and cure the leper. Are not Abana and Pharpar, the rivers of Damascus, better than all the waters of Israel? Could I not wash in them, and be clean?" So he turned and went away in a rage. But his servants came near and said to him, "My father, if the prophet had commanded you to do some great thing, would you not have done it? How much rather, then, when he says to you, 'Wash, and be clean'?" So he went down and dipped himself seven times in the Jordan, according to the word of the man of God; and his flesh was restored like the flesh of a little child, and he was clean.

Then he returned to the man of God, he and all his company, and he came and stood before him; and he said, "Behold, I know that there is no God in all the earth but in Israel."

2 Kings 5:1-15ab

2 Kings 5:1-15ab

Proper 12 (C)
Pentecost 10 (L)
Ordinary Time 17 (RC)

The Preposterous Prescription

"Go and wash in the Jordan seven times, and your flesh shall be restored." (v. 10)

Prayer: *Dear Lord, when we call on you for help, we have our own idea of the kind of help we want, when it should come, and how it should come. Help us to realize that your answer may be different from ours, and will always be more effective. Amen.*

While waiting in line at the bank, Earl, a friend I hadn't seen for some time, told me of a visit he recently had made to a doctor.

He said, "I was having some skin problems, and got an appointment with a specialist. While I was waiting in the doctor's office, I noticed a woman who went in ahead of me. Her face was quite broken out. They called me in next and put me in the little room next to hers. There were only thin partitions there, and I could hear the conversation between her and the doctor when he came in."

The doctor asked her, "Have you been using the prescription I gave you?"

The woman answered, "I'm sorry, doctor, I didn't have time to get it filled."

The doctor then said, "Then I don't have the time to treat you. I have other patients to see. Goodbye."

Earl continued by saying, "The doctor actually walked out

on her, and she had no choice but to leave. What do you think of that? It taught me a lesson, I know. If you ask for advice from someone who knows what they're talking about, you ought to be willing to follow it."

The lesson Earl learned was a good one. It doesn't make much sense to go to a doctor for treatment and then ignore it. You might as well save your money. Some folks have the notion that a doctor can wave a magic stethoscope and make them well with little or no effort on their part. It doesn't work that way. Healing is a joint effort of the patient and the physician.

Just for a moment, try to imagine what it is like when you go to a doctor for help because of a serious medical problem. After an examination, the doctor says, "I'm sorry, there is nothing I can do for you." There's no medicine, no treatment, no hope. You and I would try another doctor. But what if the answer was the same from that one and yet another?

Some of you can empathize with the person or the family that receives that kind of news. A few of you have been there yourselves, and have experienced it first hand. One man who was diagnosed as having a terminal illness, and was fortunate enough to recover, later said, "When you hear it, your heart drops through the floor. You think it can't be true. You begin to think of all the things you have planned and still want to do. Even at first you begin to go through some of those stages of Denial, Anger, Bargaining and Depression. You demand to know, "Why me, Lord?" Elizabeth Kubler-Ross, speaking at a Death and Dying Workshop, suggested that a hospital ought to have a "screaming room," where the terminally ill can express their anger and frustration.

These same feelings and emotions were undoubtedly felt by the man we meet in 2 Kings, chapter 5. This man did not have AIDS, or cancer, or a malignant tumor. But he did have a disease that in Bible times was considered disastrous. He had leprosy. His name is Naaman, commander of the army of the King of Syria.

1. A Hopeless Condition

There is no question about Naaman's qualifications as a soldier. He was a mighty man of valor. He was highly respected and regarded by the King of Syria, because through Naaman, the Lord had given victory to the Syrian forces. Leprosy, however, does not look at qualifications. It appeared that Naaman's career was over. He would no longer be able to command the army. He might have to live separately from his family. The dreaded disease presented him with a hopeless future.

What does a wife say to a husband who has no hope of getting better? What do friends say? Do they try to avoid him because they don't know what to say? You can be sure that Naaman consulted the best of the Syrian physicians. They said, "We're sorry, but there's nothing we can do."

In Naaman's house, there was a little slave girl. She had been carried off to Syria on one of the raids in Israel. She was a servant to Naaman's wife. We don't know who she was or how old she was, but she was old enough to remember the prophet in Israel who had helped many people. Sensing the cloud of gloom that had come over the family, she said to her mistress, "I wish that my master could go to the prophet who lives in Samaria! He would cure him of his disease."

Naaman's wife told her husband what the girl had said, and he told the king. The king, anxious to help, immediately said, "Go now, and I will send a letter to the King of Israel." Judging from the valuable gift of gold, silver and fine clothes that was arranged, Naaman was indeed a valuable man. All of this was put into motion because a little girl spoke up. Naaman's leprosy was supposedly incurable, but he acted on the chance, just as you or I would, that there might be a possibility of a cure.

What does all this have to do with us?

We call Naaman's illness incurable and hopeless. For all they knew in those days, there was absolutely no cure. One of the principal teachings of the Bible, in the Old Testament and in the New Testament, is that people of every generation are afflicted with the condition we call sin. You can find this condition in great personalities like David, Moses or Jacob. Ahab and Jezebel were prime examples. It's there in the New Testament as well. Jesus defined his mission by saying, "I didn't come to call the righteous, but sinners to repentance." St. Paul agonized over his inability to do the right thing, or to avoid doing the wrong thing. Sin is there like an incurable illness.

Sometimes we try to deny that this condition exists. We can be like the man in the doctor's office who comes in coughing, feverish and weak, obvious to anyone that he's really sick, who tells the doctor, "Oh, it's nothing, Doc . . . just a touch of the flu." We become experts at making excuses for our shortcomings. Even as young children we learn how to pass the buck or put the blame on someone else.

There have been many definitions of sin; among them, self-centeredness, pride, rebellion or missing the mark. Whatever your definition of sin may be, I'm sure that you have been touched by the greed or selfishness of someone else. Others, in turn, have been hurt or affected by our selfishness. "If we say we have no sin, we deceive ourselves, and the truth is not in us." (1 John 1:8) Theologically speaking, we are in a situation similar to that of Naaman. It's something we cannot get rid of by ourselves, and for which we need to seek outside help. Even if we go for help, we may say, like the woman Earl talked about, "I don't have time for that."

2. An Amazing Cure

When Naaman and his retinue arrived, the King of Israel almost pressed the panic button. He said in exasperation, "Does he think that I am God, with the power of life and death?" Kings have a measure of authority, but they do not usually heal people of leprosy. The prophet Elisha rescued the king from his dilemma. When he learned how distraught the king was, he invited the king to send the Syrian commander to him, that he may know that there is a prophet in Israel.

I wonder what Naaman thought when he pulled up his horses and chariot in front of the dwelling of Elisha. He might have felt better if it were a large, modern, spacious hospital. It was a real disappointment when a servant came out with the terse command, "Go and wash in the Jordan seven times, and your flesh shall be restored, and you shall be clean." (2 Kings 5:10)

Naaman was fit to be tied. He was angry and started to leave. This was preposterous! He had expected the prophet to come out and call on the name of his God, and wave his hands with a show of power. Naaman had come all this way with a letter and with gifts, and all he got was an insult. He had come to a specialist, and the specialist hadn't even bothered to look at him. He was offended to be asked to bathe in the Jordan River. That is like asking a man from Northern Canada, where the waters are sparkling clear and still drinkable, to take a bath in the muddy Monongahela. If all it involved was bathing, the rivers in Naaman's land were better than the Jordan. Naaman turned away in a rage.

His servants, however, saw the situation differently. They reasoned with their irate master and convinced him to try it. They said, "Sir, if the prophet had told you to do something difficult, you would have done it. Now why can't you just wash yourself as he said and be cured?" The voice of reason prevailed. Naaman swallowed his pride and went. He washed seven times in the Jordan and his flesh was restored like that of a little child!

This was an amazing cure! Who would have thought a prescription like this would take away leprosy? This was a treatment that called for faith. The faith originated in the little servant girl who innocently assumed the power of God. Because of the girl's faith, the wife told her husband, and he told the king. Naaman may have had doubts, but he went. His servants seemed to have more faith than their master, for they were the ones who convinced him to try it.

If the human condition is described as sinful, then the cure is one that washes away sin. It simply involves faith in God's way of doing it!

To many, it seems ridiculous that the Christian church still asks its converts to dip themselves, or to be sprinkled with its symbolical river, the Sacrament of Baptism. There are people who balk at this practice and refuse to take part in it. They know something is wrong, and that it is incurable, but they are too proud for that. They prefer their own ways of dealing with the fact of sin.

Baptism is God's invitation to come clean, and to find that the waters of this Sacrament actually do work! People looking for help are encouraged to believe it and to take God up on his preposterous prescription.

Many years later, a man named Peter was to tell a large throng, "Repent and be baptized every one of you in the name of Jesus Christ for the forgiveness of your sins; and you shall receive the gift of the Holy Spirit." (Acts 2:38) What Peter promised is still possible.

3. *A Strong Conviction*

Naaman returned to Elisha and wanted to thank him. He told Elisha that he now knew that there was no God in all the world but in Israel. He made arrangements to take some Israeli earth back to his home to sacrifice to this God who heals leprosy. Naaman was convinced of the power of God.

What does it take for a person to be convinced of something? In Naaman's case, it was the experience of a dramatic cure. In the case of Doubting Thomas, he insisted on seeing the Lord with his own eyes. But Jesus himself said people can believe, even without seeing. "Blessed are those who have not seen and yet believe." (John 20:29) A strong conviction comes because of what you have seen or experienced, or learned or verified from a reliable source. You and I can gain a strong conviction of faith in God's Word, knowing that our hopeless condition of sin is forgiven by an amazing cure — the grace of God in Jesus Christ.

I hope that you have a strong conviction of faith. And I also hope that you are perceptive enough to see God's help in both preposterous and in very simple ways.

Now when Elisha had fallen sick with the illness of which he was to die, Joash king of Israel went down to him, and wept before him, crying, "My father, my father! The chariots of Israel and its horsemen!" And Elisha said to him, "Take a bow and arrows"; so he took a bow and arrows. Then he said to the king of Israel, "Draw the bow"; and he drew it. And Elisha laid his hands upon the king's hands. And he said, "Open the window eastward"; and he opened it. Then Elisha said, "Shoot"; and he shot. And he said, "The Lord's arrow of victory, the arrow of victory over Syria! For you shall fight the Syrians in Aphek until you have made an end of them." And he said, "Take the arrows"; and he took them. And he said to the king of Israel, "Strike the ground with them"; and he struck three times, and stopped. Then the man of God was angry with him, and said, "You should have struck five or six times; then you would have struck down Syria until you had made an end of it, but now you will strike down Syria only three times."

So Elisha died, and they buried him.

2 Kings 13:14-20a

2 Kings 13:14-20a   *Proper 13 (C)*
                                     Pentecost 11 (L)
                              Ordinary Time 18 (RC)

Do Not Go Gentle Into That Good Night

"Then the man of God was angry with him." (v. 19)

Prayer: *O Lord, support us all the day long of this troubled life, until the shadows lengthen and the evening comes and the busy world is hushed, the fever of life is over, and our work is done. Then, Lord, in your mercy, grant us a safe lodging, and a holy rest, and peace at the last; through Jesus Christ our Lord.*[3]

Old Robert was getting more frail the summer before he died. With his emphysema, he would be puffing and fighting for breath from exertion, simply walking from the front of the house to the back. He still loved his garden, although it was nowhere near as large as it had been when he had been able to tend it properly.

One day I saw him out there, in the garden, sitting on an old wooden kitchen chair with a hoe in his hand. He was hoeing in slow motion, if that is possible. He had to be out there, taking care of those weeds. He wasn't ready to give up.

It's something like that with the man whose death is reported in today's text. Elisha, eighty years old, and ill, was given one more chance to advise the king of Israel, and to

---

[3]. *Lutheran Book of Worship,* Augsburg Publishing House, 1978, p. 158.

prophesy against their enemies. At this point in his life, he was still vitally concerned with the fortunes of his people. He, too, may have been functioning in slow motion, but he wasn't ready to give up the cause, for the people of God.

The names Elisha and Elijah are sometimes confused. We ought to be clear on whom we are talking about. Elijah came first. He was a stern, forceful, solitary man. He was the man who prayed to God for fire on Mount Carmel, as he was pitted against the prophets of Baal. He was the man who defied King Ahab and Queen Jezebel. Elijah is not the kind of man you'd find at a ball game or a birthday party.

Elisha, the man we are considering today, came after Elijah. He succeeded Elijah and was given the mantle of leadership. He was more of a gentle man, one who could be firm when necessary, but more sociable. He advised several kings during a bloody period of history. Among them were King Joram, King Jehu, King Jehoahaz and King Joash. He was a prophet for fifty years during the time of sporadic fighting with the Syrians.

Do you remember . . .

- that it was Elisha who fed a hundred men with only twenty small loaves of bread?
- that it was Elisha who retrieved an axe-head and made it float, after it had sunk?
- that it was Elisha who made a poisonous soup edible by adding a simple ingredient?
- that it was Elisha who healed Naaman, the Syrian commander, of leprosy?
- that it was Elisha who brought back to life, the son of the woman of Shunem?

Elisha had seen the fortunes of Israel go up and down. Now after fifty years of counseling kings, Elisha became sick with the illness that was to bring him to death. In verse 14, there is a brief reflection on the relation of king and prophet. His mourning shamelessly illustrates how dependent the king is on the prophet.

Now when Elisha had fallen sick with the illness of which he was to die, Joash king of Israel went down to him, and wept before him, crying, "My father, my father! The chariots of Israel and its horsemen!"

Kings don't usually make house calls. But here is an instance in which this king, Joash, recognized the imminent departure of a trusted friend and mainstay. In referring to the chariots of Israel, he was remembering those same words, uttered by Elisha, when Elijah was taken to heaven.

The old sick man ordered the king to take a bow and arrows and to get ready to shoot. He said, "Open the window to the east," and pointed the arrow in that direction, toward Syria. Elisha laid his hands on the king's hands as he shot the arrow out of the window. Elisha said, "You are the Lord's arrow, with which he will win victory over Syria. You will fight the Syrians in Aphek until you defeat them."

Then Elisha told King Joash to take the other arrows and strike the ground with them. The king did as he was told. He took the arrows, struck the ground with them three times and stopped. At this point Elisha became angry and reprimanded him. Elisha said, "You should have struck with the arrows five or six times, and then you would have had complete victory over the Syrians. As it is, you will only defeat them three times."

The king who came looking for reassurance, received only a rebuke. Instead of leaving with support, he left with a scolding. How was he to know how many times to strike the ground? The most glaring weakness of King Joash may have been that he did not share the same zealous animosity as the prophet for the enemies of God's people.

This then, is the account of the death of a prophet of God. His prophecy about the arrows came true. (2 Kings 13:25) He insisted on doing his thing right up to the last minute. His devotion to the cause never diminished. In this glimpse of Elisha near the end of his life, we can see a man who is still able to rage against evil. The manner of his death is parallel to the title of a poem written by the Welsh poet, Dylan Thomas. He wrote a poem to his father about death, titled, *Do not go gentle into that good night.* To some, death is a peaceful surrender. But not so in this poem. He describes four types of men and their various reactions to death.

1. *Wise men.* No matter how wise a man is, eventually he realizes that he was not able to change much in his life, so he does not go gentle into that good night.

2. *Good men.* Men who have led good lives look at their "goodness" and wonder what it has accomplished.

3. *Wild men.* Men who wasted their time, perhaps as hedonists, look back and see that they learned too late what life is all about.

4. *Grave men.* Men who are very serious about life also need to answer for their style of life and see what they might have missed of happiness and joy.

Dylan Thomas closes the poem by asking his father to either curse or to bless him, and ends with these words:

Do not go gentle into that good night.
Rage, rage against the dying of the light.[4]

Death is often described as quiet resignation or acceptance. Psalm 4 characterizes that impression: "In peace I will both lie down and sleep; for thou alone, O Lord, makest me dwell in safety." (Psalm 4:8) We speak of death as rest: "Blessed are the dead who die in the Lord henceforth . . . that they may rest from their labors." (Revelation 14:13) To some, death is a surrender, something you succumb to without a fight.

---

4. Dylan Thomas, *The Collected Poems of Dylan Thomas,* New Directions, 1957, p. 128.

But in the work of Dylan Thomas, it's different. In the case of Elisha, it's different.

What should a man think about on his death-bed? Should he dwell on regrets for the things he's missed? Should he feel sorry for himself? Should he curse fate and God for allowing him to reach this point?

We know what Elisha was thinking about. He was thinking about the Syrians, the enemies of God's people! When he asked King Joash to shoot an arrow, and to smash those other arrows on the ground, Elisha was still very much involved with something that had been at the heart of his life. He was deeply concerned for God's people. Let death come when it will, in the meantime, he is fiercely devoted to seeing God's people prevail! Elisha wasn't just sitting there waiting to die. What filled his soul through life was also filling his soul at the time of his death.

How many of us have a passionate desire to see God's will prevail? Do we care? What will we be thinking about when our time comes? Will we just want to be comfortable? Will we just want someone else close by? Will we be afraid and think only of ourselves?

The key to understanding Elisha's attitude toward his approaching death is this: he had a passionate desire to bring about God's will. It may be akin to that mysterious power that we call "the will to live." Some people say, "I'm tired and I'm ready to quit," while others say, "I'm angry that I have to quit; there is so much I still want to do."

If this is true for an individual, is it not true on a larger scale as well? Isn't it possible for a group of people to have a passionate desire to bring about God's will? Isn't it possible for a church? Isn't it possible for a nation? Or for humanity? We often hear it said, "I've done my share, let someone else take over now." Or we hear a meek voice saying, "It doesn't matter what I do."

It *does* matter! It *is* important! It *does* make a difference!

Take this concept from the Old Testament and place it in

the New. You and I are called to care about the Gospel! You and I are called to be loyal to Christ! You and I are called to help bring about God's will! Now if I said that we are called to be "fanatics," you wouldn't like to hear that, and I wouldn't like to say it. The word "fanatic" has a bad connotation in our culture. A fanatic is a person who is unreasonably enthusiastic, overly zealous. In religious circles, a fanatic is one whose extreme zeal and piety goes far beyond what is reasonable.

Yet we are the people who are called to take up the cross. Is there anything more fanatical than that? We are called to go the second mile, and to pray for our enemies and those who persecute us. Is that reasonable behavior?

Sometimes I think that we have only begun to scratch the tip of the iceberg we call commitment. We talk about it, and pretend to be doing it, but seldom go so far as to stake our lives on it.

Ultimately there is only one reason why people should do anything in the way of faith. That is because they have seen the overwhelming love of God in Jesus Christ! That love is worth everything. Jesus Christ loved this world with a passion. He loved the world — and that means you and me — enough to go as far as he could . . . until he died doing it. That kind of love is amazing and wonderful and awesome. That kind of love is inspiring enough, not to go gentle into that good night, but to make every moment here count.

The word that came to Jeremiah from the Lord: "Arise, and go down to the potter's house, and there I will let you hear my words." So I went down to the potter's house, and there he was working at his wheel. And the vessel he was making of clay was spoiled in the potter's hand, and he reworked it into another vessel, as it seemed good to the potter to do.

Then the word of the Lord came to me: "O house of Israel, can I not do with you as this potter has done? says the Lord. Behold, like the clay in the potter's hand, so are you in my hand, O house of Israel. If at any time I declare concerning a nation or a kingdom, that I will pluck up and break down and destroy it, and if that nation, concerning which I have spoken, turns from its evil, I will repent of the evil that I intended to do to it. And if at any time I declare concerning a nation or a kingdom that I will build and plant it, and if it does evil in my sight, not listening to my voice, then I will repent of the good which I had intended to do to it. Now, therefore, say to the men of Judah and the inhabitants of Jerusalem: 'Thus says the Lord, Behold, I am shaping evil against you and devising a plan against you. Return, every one from his evil way, and amend your ways and your doings.' "

Jeremiah 18:1-11

Jeremiah 18:1-11 *Proper 14 (C)*
Pentecost 12 (L)
Ordinary Time 19 (RC)

The Focus of Fitness

"Return, every one from his evil way, and amend your ways and your doings." (v. 11)

Prayer: *Lord, you have made it plain that you care what we do with our lives. You are pleased when we seek to do your will, and you grieve for us when we ignore it. Speak to us in this time of worship and enable us to re-discover the joy and the blessing of doing it your way. Amen*

Has there been a more popular pastime in recent years, than that of "getting in shape"? One magazine called it "America's Health and Fitness Craze." Everywhere you look, people are jogging, walking, or running. Some prefer to play with a paddle or a racket. Others lift weights or swim at a health club. Some order an apparatus with which you can make your living room into a gymnasium, an exercise machine or a device you can use in the privacy of your own home. It seems that everyone is interested in getting in shape.

It may be that we have developed so many labor-saving devices and appliances that we now have to buy something to begin using our muscles again! If we could bring someone back to life from 100 years ago, to see our popular interest in exercise, what might they think? Back in those days, there wasn't time or energy to take 45 minutes jogging or lifting, just for the sake of exercise. They might consider us a little bit daffy.

Along with the desire for fitness are the many suggested

diets by which to lose weight. "Getting in shape" for many people means losing ten, twenty, thirty or more pounds. Many of the plans claim that theirs is the "easy" way. But is there an easy way? Some of you have tried it, and you know how "easy" it is.

Physical fitness is a popular theme because most people are interested in a better quality of life. Who can argue with that? We could list a number of good reasons why physical fitness is so important. It involves the following:

a. When you are physically fit, you feel better and can function better in all aspects of life.

b. You'll have more confidence and be more sure of yourself. You'll feel good about yourself.

c. Fitness means that you have a good chance of living longer and being able to enjoy it.

Without saying it outright, most of those who want us to spend our money on fitness subtly suggest that being in shape is the best way to be more sexy!

This reminds me of the man who stopped to weigh himself on a weighing machine. He put the coin in, drew the ticket out, and was obviously pleased. He handed it to his wife, and she read it aloud: "You are dynamic, a born leader, handsome, admired by women for your personality." She added, "It's got your weight wrong, too."

Whether you boldly change your diet; or scrooch back and forth in front of your television on one of those exercise machines; or faithfully jog three miles every morning; getting in shape is one of America's great pastimes. Some might call it an obsession. But who can argue against health and fitness? The alternative is certainly not very appealing.

There is a reason for this digression to focus on fitness. The reason lies in the last verse of the text for today,

Jeremiah 18:11: "Return, every one of you from his evil way, and amend your ways and your doings." That is a call to fitness. In Jeremiah's eyes, it applies to everyone of us. No one is perfect.

Jeremiah, one of the major prophets, lived during the time of the destruction of Jerusalem, 640 to 587 B.C. He made use of object lessons, such as a loincloth, (Jeremiah 13:1-11); wine jars, (Jeremiah 13:12); pottery, (Jeremiah 18:1-11); a broken jar, (Jeremiah 19:1-13); and figs (Jeremiah 24:1-10).

In the verses before us, Jeremiah was instructed to visit the potter's house and to watch him at work. Imagine the potter sitting at the wheel. The wheel is about the size of an old piano stool, going around and around. Today, the potter flips a switch, and the wheel turns, powered by an electric motor. In Jeremiah's day, the mechanism was turned by hand or foot, crude to our standards, but still the same principle.

As the potter puts the lump of clay on the turntable, it is constantly worked by hand. Water is sprinkled on it to keep the lump soft and pliable. The turntable is there for a reason. If you have ever tried to shape something out of clay by using your hands only, you have probably discovered that there were thick parts and thin parts. It is lumpy and doesn't hold together. By placing it on a turn-table, it is possible to work it by hand and to get a uniform thickness both inside and outside of the vessel you are forming.

It may happen that the potter is dissatisfied with what is there, and will pick up the lump, make it into a ball, and start over. As long as the clay is soft and pliable, it can be reworked. But if there is a dry spot or some foreign substance, then the clay will need to be reworked and begun again.

As Jeremiah watched the potter, the word of the Lord came to him. God is like a potter who can decide to do one of two things with the clay. One is, he decides to rework the lump and to start over. But then he looks again, changes his mind and decides to keep it after all. The other alternative approach is, he decides to make a very nice piece out of the clay, but the clay does not cooperate and has to be reworked.

These two approaches apply to God and his feelings toward his people. One thing that might happen is that God would say, "I am not pleased with my people. I think I will destroy them." But then the people repent and turn from their evil, and God does not destroy them.

The other alternative is when God intends to make his people great, but they disregard his Word and disobey him. Having no other choice, he destroys them and starts over.

This principle is similar to the experience that dozens of young people have in making preparations for their exhibits at the County Fair. Trudy is a good example. She is in 4-H. She has some plaid material, and she's making a suit. As she cuts the material, she says, "Oh, no! This doesn't look right. I'm going to have to start over!" But the next morning she looks at it again and says to herself, "This isn't quite so bad. In fact, if I just move this seam over and change this pleat, it will work!" This is like what happens when God decides to destroy, but his people repent, and he decides not to destroy them.

But another girl named Nancy is also working on an outfit. As she begins, she anticipates that this will be the best piece of work she has ever done. However, as she starts in, it becomes evident that this material and this design simply are not going to work. She will have to set it aside and try something else. This too, is what happens when God wants his people to be faithful, but they turn and disobey him.

The key question for the lump of clay or the piece of material is, Is it going to work? Is it going to be worthwhile? That is also the question God asks about us. Are these people going to shape up? Are they going to heed my word? Are they going to repent and turn from their evil ways? Or are they going to continue on their merry way, on the road that leads to destruction?

Let me pose a couple of questions, in regard to Jeremiah's observation of the potter.

1. Does it really make any difference what we do?

Doesn't God know the end of the story? There's not much we can do to change it. He knows where we're going to end up, and where this world is going to end up. So does it make any difference what we do?

The answer is yes. Otherwise, the Lord would not have provided for his Word to be spread and shared. If it didn't make a difference, we wouldn't need a church. We wouldn't need a Bible. We wouldn't need people to witness for Christ. We could let the world run on to its own destiny on a preprogrammed script.

Jesus Christ came to tell us that it makes a tremendous difference what we do with our lives. God cares what we do with our lives. One of the devil's most effective approaches to present-day people, is the innocent question, "So what?"

- People are starving. So what? Some have always been starving.
- People are killing themselves with drugs. So what? This is nothing new.
- People are victims of injustice. So what? As long as it isn't me, what do I care?

The Son of God showed us how to care. He became one of us; he identified with us; he lived among us, laughed and cried among us, and died among us. Through Christ, God has changed human history to give hope in place of despair; life in place of death; promise in place of hopelessness; mercy in place of condemnation.

2. What is Jeremiah's advice to Christians today?

The advice is simple: "Return, every one of you from his evil way, and amend your ways and your doings."

This is the Old Testament way of saying, "Get in shape." Be bold enough to change your lifestyle. Don't just be contented to watch others from the sidelines. Ask: What can I do, for God's sake?

Today's Gospel from Luke 12 speaks about being ready,

watching for the coming of the master. The problem for us is that sometimes God seems far away, and far removed from us.

In the movie "Love and Death," Woody Allen plays a man called Boris, and Diane Keaton plays a young woman named Sonya. At one point in the movie, Boris asks Sonya, "What if there is no god? What if we're just a bunch of absurd people who are running around with no rhyme or reason?"

Sonya replies, "But if there is no god, then life has no meaning. Why go on living? Why not just commit suicide?"

Boris, a bit flustered, says, "Well, let's not get hysterical. I could be wrong. I'd hate to blow my brains out and then read in the papers that they found something."

In this movie, Woody Allen puts in a humorous form a question that lies deep within our souls. If God really exists, why doesn't he demonstrate his existence? "If God would only give me some clear sign . . ." said Boris, ". . . like making a large deposit in my name at a Swiss bank, or if I could just see a miracle . . . a burning bush, or see the seas part, or my Uncle Sasha pick up a check, or . . . if God would just cough!"

God has come. He came in a man named Jesus. He paid a great price in his death, and in his resurrection he lives and rules with power. His message to us is similar to that of Jeremiah: "Return, every one of you!"

O Lord, thou hast deceived me,
*   and I was deceived;*
thou art stronger than I,
*   and thou hast prevailed.*
I have become a laughingstock all
*   the day;*
*   every one mocks me.*
For whenever I speak, I cry out,
*   I shout, "Violence and destruction!"*
For the word of the Lord has become
*   for me*
*   a reproach and derision all day*
*   long.*
If I say, "I will not mention him,
*   or speak any more in his*
*   name,"*
there is in my heart as it were a
*   burning fire*
*   shut up in my bones,*
and I am weary with holding it
*   in,*
*   and I cannot.*
For I hear many whispering.
*   Terror is on every side!*
"Denounce him! Let us denounce
*   him!"*
*   say all my familiar friends,*
*   watching for my fall.*
"Perhaps he will be deceived,
*   then we can overcome him,*
*   and take our revenge on*
*   him.*
But the Lord is with me as a dread
*   warrior;*
*   therefore my persecutors will*
*   stumble,*
*   they will not overcome me.*
They will be greatly shamed,
*   for they will not succeed.*

*Their eternal dishonor
  will never be forgotten.
O Lord of hosts, who triest the
    righteous,
  who seest the heart and the
    mind,
let me see thy vengeance upon
    them.
  for to thee have I committed
    my cause.
Sing to the Lord;
  praise the Lord!
For he has delivered the life of
    the needy
  from the hand of evildoers.*

Jeremiah 20:7-13

Jeremiah 20:7-13 *Proper 15 (C)*
Pentecost 13 (L)
Ordinary Time 20 (RC)

I Never Promised You a Rose Garden

"The word of the Lord has become for me a reproach and derision all day long." (v. 8)

Prayer: *Lord, you have called us to a faith that is much more than a sentimental security blanket. You have challenged us to live out what we say we believe. You never said it would be easy. Give us the courage to stand up and be counted, and also the courage to keep standing after we have been counted.*

"I beg your pardon; I never promised you a rose garden. Along with the sunshine, there's got to be a little rain, sometime." This is the refrain of a song that was popular in the 70s.

The lyrics continue with the singer telling his sweetheart that he could promise her things like big diamond rings, the moon, or the world on a silver platter; but the only thing he can give is himself. He cannot promise "a rose garden," because life is unpredictable and there are certain to be difficult times.

In a different setting, the same phrase *I never promised you a rose garden*, is also the title of a novel written by Hannah Green. It is the story of a young woman, named Deborah, who is mentally ill. She has lost touch with reality and lives in a dream world. One reviewer says that Deborah is courageous and heroic, yet she might be any one of us. Her story gives belief and promise to those who are concerned with the human spirit. No rose garden is offered to Deborah, yet she slowly fights her way back to reality, to a world that is often harsh and challenging. It is the story of one young woman's successful fight for health, and of the others around her who wage their own battles, sometimes winning, sometimes losing.

No one can promise you that your life will be pleasant, comfortable, free from stress and from aches and pains all the way through. No one can guarantee that your life will be happy, successful or that it will fulfill your dreams. There is an inherent risk in being born and living. Every day's news underscores the hazards.

An esteemed professor in a seminary was lecturing to his church history class. He had just described some of the martyrs of the early church; people who lost their lives because of their faithfulness to the gospel. He closed his book and looked the students in the eye, and said, "You know, things haven't changed a whole lot in many parts of the world. Some of you may be called on to defend the faith, and to lay your reputation on the line. It is not beyond the realm of imagination that some of you may one day be in the position to die for your faith."

God never promised that it would be easy. He promised to be with you, but not that it's always going to be pleasant and sweet.

Now what does all this have to do with Jeremiah 20:7-13?

Of the text we are considering today, one commentator said this: "This is one of the most powerful and impressive passages in the whole of prophetic literature." That's quite a statement. He adds, "No other passage in all the prophetic literature expresses so clearly as this, the prophet's sense of divine compulsion to his task."[5]

---

5. *Interpreter's Bible,* Abingdon Press, Vol. 5, pp. 971-972.

Here is a lament, a complaint, a prayer. Here is Jeremiah, baring his soul. It's almost as if we were walking by Jeremiah's room, the door is open, and we hear him talking to God. Jeremiah describes himself as being *compelled, confronted* and *committed.*

1. Compelled (Verses 7-9)

The prophet says, "God has deceived me . . . I have become a laughing-stock and a joke." People are making fun of him because he proclaims God's message, shouting "Violence and destruction!"

One of Norman Rockwell's classic Saturday Evening Post covers shows a boy all dressed up in a suit, pushing a baby buggy. He is obviously unhappy, especially since two other boys are passing by, wearing their baseball uniforms, mocking him. No one likes to be laughed at. Garrison Keillor, reporting the news from Lake Wobegon, told in one of his broadcasts, how it felt to go to the county fair as a young boy, all dressed up and carrying a Bible. One of the first things he and the others did was to find a sack for their Bibles, so they wouldn't be so obvious. It reminds me of the boy who went to camp, whose mother was worried that he might be ridiculed if the other boys knew he was a Christian. When he returned, she asked him about it, and he said, "There was no problem, Mom; nobody found out that I was Christian."

Have you ever felt foolish for being a Christian? Other people don't seem to worry about what is right or wrong. They just go on their merry way. Sometimes they want you to join in their fun. It seems innocent enough, but you wonder. You don't feel right about it. You feel as though you don't belong.

Bearing the name of Christ does involve responsibility. At times, it becomes frustrating to know just how much of the world one is responsible for. Conscientious Christians are sitting ducks for guilt feelings. It seems that whatever we do, it isn't quite enough. The transient who comes to the door of the church, and needs gas, or a meal, or a place to stay, knows what Christianity is supposed to be all about.

The prophet Jeremiah describes his compelling urgency to speak the Word of God. He says, "There is in my heart as it were a burning fire shut up in my bones, and I am weary with holding it in, and I cannot." Sometimes we try to put that compelling urgency out of our minds, and we succeed. Sometimes the only burning fire we feel is when we ate too much at the last church potluck.

Some of our compulsive speech may not come from divine motivation, but from anger, quick reactions and hasty judgments. We have no business claiming God's inspiration for our childish outbursts of anger. What Jeremiah is talking about, is the compelling necessity to speak the word of God which may well produce enemies. People simply won't like it, and they will vent their dislike on the speaker. But for God's prophet, that's the way it is.

When I think of our usual reticence to speak an uncomfortable word, or to be in a place where we are not appreciated, I think of the following conversation:

"No one at school likes me," said the son to his mother. "The kids don't, and the teachers feel the same way. I'd like to stay home."

"You have to go," insisted his mother. "You're not sick. You have a lot to learn. Besides, you're 46 years old. You're the principal, and you have to go to school."

2. *Confronted* (Verses 10-11)

The word "confronted" points in two directions. On the one hand, Jeremiah's enemies are confronting him with threats and revenge. On the other hand, the Lord confronts the enemies and causes them to stumble. Being confronted with enemies is not a pleasant experience. I remember a boy in elementary school who somehow drew abuse and meanness from the other boys. As I look back, I'm not sure if it was his personality, or mannerisms or something else. But he was a victim time and time again. Life must have been miserable for that boy. He was the object of derision.

Such is the experience of Jeremiah. He sees his enemies and some of his former friends waiting to pounce on him. They are watching for his downfall, just waiting for him to slip. The word "terror" is used to describe the animosity toward Jeremiah. Although the term "terrorist" seems to have become commonly used only in recent years, the significance of the term has been around ever since people discovered how to frighten one another.

Even if you don't have outright enemies, it is possible to feel very much alone. There may have been times in your life when you have felt no one cares. A woman in a large office was trying to do her job, but finally quit the job because she couldn't stand the constant criticism from her boss. There are many subtle and effective ways for people to mistreat each other.

Jeremiah doesn't need to fear his enemies, because the Lord is with him as a "dread warrior." Like a strong, big brother, the Lord looks after his own. The persecutors will stumble; they can't win. You've heard of a "No win" situation. This is the way it is when people try to oppose God. The advice of Gamaliel is still valid: "If this plan or this undertaking is of men, it will fail; but if it is of God, you will not be able to overthrow them. You might even be found opposing God!" (Acts 5:39)

3. *Committed* (Verses 12-13)

A woman in the hospital, facing several weeks of chemotherapy treatments, was in good spirits. She said, "I've decided that I can't carry this load all by myself. It's in the Lord's hands. Whatever his will is, is mine also."

There is relief, and peace that defies understanding, when you put something in the Lord's hands. Jeremiah said, "for to thee have I committed my cause." One version of the Bible translates it, "I've laid my case before you."

The act of commitment has sound precedent. Jesus himself said, "Father, into your hands I commit my spirit." (Luke 23:46) He committed his way to the Father in the Garden of Gethsemane, saying "Your will, not mine be done." The advice given in Psalm 37, "Commit your way to the Lord," is among the best advice given for tension, anxiety or worry.

The Lord has not promised you or me a rose garden. He has put us in this harsh world, where we must co-exist with problems derived from hate, jealousy, pride and greed. Our hope lies in what the Lord has promised. He has promised to be with each one of us, no matter what, "I will never fail you nor forsake you," (Hebrews 13:5), says the Lord.

In that same year, at the beginning of the reign of Zedekiah king of Judah, in the fifth month of the fourth year, Hananiah the son of Azzur, the prophet from Gibeon, spoke to me in the house of the Lord, in the presence of the priests and all the people, saying, "Thus says the Lord of hosts, the God of Israel: I have broken the yoke of the king of Babylon. Within two years I will bring back to this place all the vessels of the Lord's house, which Nebuchadnezzar king of Babylon took away from this place and carried to Babylon. I will also bring back to this place Jeconiah the son of Jehoiakim, king of Judah, and all the exiles from Judah who went to Babylon, says the Lord, for I will break the yoke of the king of Babylon."

Then the prophet Jeremiah spoke to Hananiah the prophet in the presence of the priests and all the people who were standing in the house of the Lord; and the prophet Jeremiah said, "Amen! May the Lord do so; may the Lord make the words which you have prophesied come true, and bring back to this place from Babylon the vessels of the house of the Lord, and all the exiles. Yet hear now this word which I speak in your hearing and in the hearing of all the people. The prophets who preceded you and me from ancient times prophesied war, famine, and pestilence against many countries and great kingdoms. As for the prophet who prophesies peace, when the word of that prophet comes to pass, then it will be known that the Lord has truly sent the prophet."

Jeremiah 28:1-9

Jeremiah 28:1-9

Proper 16 (C)
Pentecost 14 (L)
Ordinary Time 21 (RC)

The Cracked Crystal Ball

"Thus says the Lord of hosts?" (v. 2)

Prayer: *Lord, we know that your ways are often not our ways, and that our ways are often not your ways. Because you are wiser than we are, give us the grace to admit that we don't know all the answers.*

Think of a crystal ball and you probably think of a fortuneteller. But today, crystal balls are not limited to fortunetellers.

Economists have them.
Meteorologists are said to have them.
Poll takers are suspected of borrowing them.
Some politicians wish they had one.
The faithful at the race track would pay a premium for one.

The only problem is that most of the crystal balls available today are cracked. They just don't work right. The voice which assures us of one thing today, too often has to change its forecast tomorrow. Banks have devised something like a hymn board, on which you can change the numbers each week, to keep up with fluctuating interest rates. It is always risky to predict or to try to guarantee anything in the future, except perhaps those sobering reports issued by the highway department before each holiday weekend.

The art of prediction has always been associated with the people we call prophets. The prophets of the Scriptures, however, never needed crystal balls. They had something much more reliable. Their prophecy was based on the Word of God.

The art of prediction has always been associated with the people we call prophets. The people of God ought to be able to distinguish a legitimate prophet from a false one; but it is difficult, especially when the false ones look and sound so much like the real ones.

The matter of false prophecy confronts us in today's text. Now you may not get terribly excited about a debate between two men with odd-sounding names, who both claimed to be speaking the Word of God in their little corner of the world, many years ago. But the substance of their claim is something quite contemporary. This is a matter that is of concern to every Christian. Who speaks for God today? Whom can we believe? Who is speaking the truth? Are there voices that may be leading us astray?

Recently a brochure came through the mail, containing some "Solemn Prophetic Warnings," written by Stanley Frodsham. He stated this warning about modern-day seducers and false prophets:

> *Do you think a seducer will brandish a new heresy and flaunt it before the people? He will speak the words of righteousness and truth and will appear as a minister of light, declaring the Word.*

Seeing that, I have to admit that it makes sense. The best of the false prophets are those who appear most authentic. Some wolves have learned how to tailor and to wear sheep's clothing so well that few can tell the difference.

Jesus gave his classic advice in the Sermon on the Mount. "Beware of false prophets who come to you in sheep's clothing but inwardly are ravenous wolves. You will know them by their fruits." (Matthew 7:15-16) The problem in our instant-oriented and mobile society, is that we don't have the time to wait around for the fruits, nor do we care to wait for them. By the time we find time to examine the fruits, the prophet, like the home-run ball hit by the Detroit Tigers, and described in the words of radio announcer, Ernie Harwell, has "long gone."

There may be an easier way to detect a false prophet in our time. The false prophet is one who will:
   a. Tell us what we like to hear.
   b. Tell us what we want to hear.
   c. Tell us everything is going to be all right, even when it's not.

1. Tell Us What We Like to Hear

These two prophets from the past are named Hananiah and Jeremiah. By just hearing the names, your opinion may be prejudiced on the side of Jeremiah, for we already know that he was a man of God. Otherwise, there wouldn't be a book named after him in the Bible. Christians have no reason to question Jeremiah's authenticity. His prophecy was not popularly accepted, and because he said some things that sounded foreboding, some called him the weeping prophet.

Hananiah, on the other hand, looked into the future and announced that God's people would be back from exile in two years. The yoke of the king of Babylon would be broken, and the holy vessels which had been taken from the temple would be returned. Everything would be as it should be. This was news that the hearers would have welcomed. It was prophecy of a positive nature, implying victory and restoration. The only thing wrong was, according to Jeremiah, it was not to be so.

In the previous chapter (Jeremiah 27), Jeremiah, at the Lord's command, had made an ox yoke, and wore it before the ambassadors who had come to Jerusalem. He gave them a charge to take back to their respective kings. The yoke was Nebuchadnezzar's yoke which the Lord placed on their necks. They were to wear it or face destruction. Jeremiah was saying that they must wear the yoke of the king of Babylon. Hananiah was saying that that yoke would be broken and everything brought back to normal in two years. One of them was telling the people what they liked to hear, and the other was not.

No one likes to hear a prophecy of subjection or servitude. Yet Jeremiah saw this as God's will. That view goes a long way toward explaining Jeremiah's seemingly unpatriotic and defeatist attitude in the years that followed.

2. Tell Us What We Want to Hear

There is a remarkable short story, written by Pulitzer Prize winning author, James Agee, called *A Mother's Tale*. In the story, he raises the issues of credibility and destiny. It's a story written from the viewpoint of beef cattle.

A mother cow, out on the range, is asked by her young ones, "Why have men come to drive away some of the cattle? Where are they going?" The young are excited and curious, wanting to go along, not wanting to be left out. In response to their repeated questions, she tells them what she has heard passed down from her great grandmother. She tells them about the train, the iron bars of the railroad, the long trip of the cattle squeezed into box cars, the unloading at the stock yards, and about the final destination, the slaughter house.

One of the cattle which had been to the slaughter house, had miraculously escaped, even after being struck on the head and assumed to be dead. This one returned walking back the many miles, following the railroad back to the range. Showing the severe scars of his ordeal, he tried to convince the others of what he had seen and been through. He urged them to rebel or to try to escape from the men who would take them away. Some believed him, others thought he was crazy, some wanted to see for themselves.

Her son was one who couldn't quite believe all this. He wanted to see for himself. He thought if it was true, then he would be prepared. He said to himself, ". . . the one I will charge is The Man With The Hammer. I'll put Him and His Hammer out of the way forever, and that will make me an even better hero than The One Who Came Back."[6] His ideas

---

6. *The Collected Short Prose of James Agee*, Robert Fitzgerald, ed., Houghton Mifflin Co., 1968, p. 243.

were impressive, but destined to fail. He heard only what he wanted to hear.

The story ends on a plaintive note when one of her little calves asks his mother, "What's a train?"

What we hear and what we want to hear are not always the same. Paul, writing to Timothy, says, "For the time is coming when people will not endure sound teaching, but having itching ears they will accumulate for themselves teachers to suit their own likings, and will turn away from listening to the truth and wander into myths." (2 Timothy 4:3-4)

3. Tell Us Everything is Going to Be All Right

Jeremiah responds to Hananiah's rosy prophecy, by saying, "I wish it were so!" All of us like to hear someone say, "Everything is going to be all right!" But that wish and that word of Hananiah was not destined to come true yet. The Lord had decreed a time of exile.

Jeremiah then gave his interpretation of what is involved in true prophecy. He said, "As for the prophet who prophesies peace, when the word of that prophet comes to pass, then it will be known that the Lord has truly sent the prophet." (Jeremiah 28:9) Many prophets foretell destruction. But the real test of a prophet is whether he can see the Lord bringing about peace down the road. Peace is much more difficult to achieve than war.

Neither you nor I need a crystal ball to tell us what is coming. We have the Word of God and that is sufficient. In his wisdom, the Lord has chosen not to reveal the future to satisfy our curiosity. He assures us that we do not have to face the future alone, for he is beside us.

Gerhard Frost has written the following words as a simple reflection of his faith.

I Will Remember

*Morning has broken,
long shadows are receding;
time for today's resolution:
With the Spirit's help
I will remember that the toughest,
most resilient and tenacious,
most stubborn and unyielding
fact that I'll encounter this day
is the eternal and all-embracing
love of God.*

With a God like this, and his caring love, you'll never need a crystal ball.

The word of the Lord came to me again: "What do you mean by repeating this proverb concerning the land of Israel, 'The fathers have eaten our sour grapes, and the children's teeth are set on edge'? As I live, says the Lord God, this proverb shall no more be used by you in Israel. Behold, all souls are mine; the soul of the father as well as the soul of the son is mine; the soul that sins shall die.

If a man is righteous and does what is lawful and right — if he does not eat upon the mountains or lift up his eyes to the idols of the house of Israel, does not defile his neighbor's wife or approach a woman in her time of impurity, does not oppress any one, but restores to the debtor his pledge, commits no robbery, gives his bread to the hungry and covers the naked with a garment, does not lend at interest or take any increase, withholds his hand from iniquity, executes true justice between man and man, walks in my statutes, and is careful to observe my ordinances — he is righteous, he shall surely live, says the Lord God.

"Yet you say, 'The way of the Lord is not just.' Hear now, O house of Israel: Is my way not just? Is it not your ways that are not just? When a righteous man turns away from his righteousness and commits iniquity, he shall die for it; for the iniquity which he has committed he shall die. Again, when a wicked man turns away from the wickedness he has committed and does what is lawful and right, he shall save his life. Because he considered and turned away from all the transgressions which he had committed, he shall surely live, he shall not die. Yet the house of Israel says, 'The way of the Lord is not just.' O house of Israel, are my ways not just? Is it not your ways that are not just?"

Ezekiel 18:1-9, 25-29

Ezekiel 18:1-9, 25-29 *Proper 17 (C)*
Pentecost 15 (L)
Ordinary Time 22 (RC)

. . . and Justice for All

"Is my way not just?" (v. 25)

Prayer: *O Lord, keep us from making hasty judgments until all the facts are in. Then let us temper our judgments with mercy, as you do to us. Amen*

Husbands and wives were invited to a Prayer Breakfast, sponsored by the local Kiwanis Club. After the opening prayer and the Pledge of Allegiance, one woman remarked, "I don't think I've said the Pledge of Allegiance since I was in grade school." Many of us have learned the Pledge of Allegiance to the Flag in elementary school. After saying it daily for several years, it becomes part of us.

The Pledge of Allegiance was first used in 1892, as a patriotic expression, when Francis Bellamy, an associate editor of a magazine, came up with it. President Benjamin Harrison had asked for expressions in appreciation of America that year, in honor of the 400th anniversary of Columbus' exploratory voyage.

As a theme for these selected verses from Ezekiel 18, you will think with me about the last phrase of the Pledge of Allegiance, ". . . and Justice for all."

Applied Justice

Every nation and community practices some kind of justice. In our own country we have laws, courts, judges and juries. We have rights and appeal procedures; we have fines and incarceration. Our system has city, county, district, federal and supreme courts. Justice works, but certainly not always perfectly. Even though we are at times skeptical of the system and possible abuses, I don't know many who would be willing to trade our system for something else.

Our judicial system seems to be either praised or criticized, depending on how you are affected. We hear it said, "If you have enough money, you can hire expert legal counsel and stay out of jail." Some claim it's possible to get off easier by knowing the right people. Regardless of the defects in the system, most of us no doubt approve when we hear of the arrest of a person selling illegal drugs. We applaud the law enforcement officers who find the hit-and-run driver who ran over a child, or who risk their lives dealing with someone who has gone berserk.

Distorted Justice

The theme of justice is portrayed vividly in the book, *The Ox-Bow Incident*, written by Walter Van Tilburg Clark. It's a "Western" story about cowboys, rustlers and a lynching, and the psychological effects on the men involved.

In the story, a report is brought in by a galloping rider that rustlers have stolen forty head of cattle and that a cowhand named Kinkaid was shot in the head. Several men immediately organize a posse to go and find the rustlers and to bring them to justice — the "lynching kind" of justice.

As they gather, one man urges the group to wait and go through the proper channels of the sheriff and the judge. The leader, a man named Bartlett says he's had enough rustling. He replies:

> *Do we have rights as men and cattle or don't we? If we wait for Judge Tyler, there won't be any cattle left in the meadows by the time we get justice.*[7]

Walter Van Tilburg Clark, *The Ox-Bow Incident,* Time, Inc., 1962, p. 43.

Bartlett continues, asking "What is justice?" raising his voice higher:

> *Is it justice that we sweat ourselves sick and old every damned day of the year to make a handful of honest dollars and then lose it all in one night because Judge Tyler says we have to fold our hands and wait for his eternal justice?*[8]

As it was, there weren't many verified facts about the incident. There was the report of rustling, but no one had actually seen the man who was shot. But the group was riled up enough and left. It turned out that the posse did find the suspects. Those accused had cattle with them, which they said they had purchased, but had no bill of sale. One suspect had an incriminating weapon with him which he said he had found. The posse was convinced that they were guilty and hung the three men.

Moments after the lynching, they discovered that they had lynched the wrong men. This group was innocent. Any evidence they had was coincidental and could be explained. The Ox-Bow Incident kind of justice is scary, when you realize how easily human passion can get in the way of logic, reasoning, facts and truth.

Before we condemn these fictional cattle men completely, ask yourself:
- How many times have I jumped to conclusions?
- How many times have I scolded my children before knowing all the facts?
- How many times have I blamed someone else for a problem before discovering that it was my fault?

We all want justice, especially when we feel we're right, or when we feel we may have been wronged. Someone has pointed out that our idea of justice is often "just us." We care little what happens to the other person. Ezekiel points out that what people perceive as justice is not always the same as what God enacts as justice.

---

8. ibid.

Moral Justice

Instead of taking personal responsiblity for what was happening, people were blaming their ancestors. The proverb of sour grapes is simply a complaint filed by the Israelites, demanding to know why they should have to suffer for the sins of their parents. Ezekiel assures them that they are responsible for their own sins.

The prophet gives an interesting thumbnail sketch of a righteous person in verses 5-9. Here are the qualifications:
The righteous person:
- Does not look wistfully at idols;
- Does not eat sacrifices offered at forbidden shrines;
- Does not seduce another person's spouse;
- Does not cheat or steal from anyone;
- Does not charge others unjustly;
- Does return what was given as a pledge for a loan;
- Does feed the hungry and give clothing to the naked;
- Does practice fair dealing among associates.

Such a person is righteous, and will live, says the Lord. Can't we all go along with that? Something deep within us says that the person who has done right deserves a reward. Isn't that why we have medals and blue ribbons, scouting badges and certificates? One of the most effective ways we have in our society, to honor people who have done and given their best, is recognition! It means rewarding a person for what he or she is worth. In the same way, it seems that when we do good for God, he ought to smile at us, pat us on the back and say, "I'm so proud of you!"

If that were all there is to religion, what some earlier theologians called "works-righteousness," then our teaching and our preaching would be vastly different. We could eliminate every reference to human depravity and forgiveness, and stress instead the "human potential" for good. We would not need a Savior or a Cross if we could do it ourselves.

God's Justice

In the book *Anatomy of a Murder*, by Robert Traver, the judge in the story, in a reflective moment, philosophizes about humanity. He says, "Man is the only animal that laughs and weeps, for he is the only animal that is struck by the difference between what things are and what they ought to be."

Ezekiel is well aware of that difference, as he speaks the word of God. God's justice takes into account the way things are and the way they ought to be. His chief concern is the urgent appeal stated in verse 31. (Ezekiel 18:31): "Cast away from you all the transgressions which you have committed against me, and get yourselves a new heart and a new spirit!"

We don't need to worry about God's ultimate judgment. We can trust him to deliver justice for all. Our challenge is to live in response to his love. In that age-old debate about faith and good works, we know that neither one is excluded. It's like the old Scotchman who had a rowboat to take people across the river. On one of his oars was painted the word "Faith" and on the other, the word "Works." When a passenger asked about those words. he showed them what would happen if he used only one of them. The boat, with one oar, started to go in a circle. It takes both to get somewhere.

I happen to be driving a car with a fuel-injection system. A few months ago it began to lose power. The fuel-injectors had to be replaced. In the case of my car, this cost over a hundred dollars. The mechanic asked if I had been using a cheaper grade of gasoline, and I admitted that I had. He suggested using a better fuel to avoid this problem in the future. To save a few cents on a gallon, I had been putting something in that was not good for the engine.

This same principle applies to our bodies and our minds. What kind of junk do we put into our bodies that clogs up the system? What cheap things do we put into our minds? Fuel-injectors can be replaced, but not the body or the mind.

God cares what we do. He cares how we live. He cares so

much that he did something to make it clear. He didn't want anyone to miss it or mistake it. He sent his Son to suffer injustice on the Cross, in order to show his love. That love is so overwhelming that "I scarce can take it in!" He holds his arms out to us. He doesn't want anyone to perish. We don't have to worry how he's going to treat us. Let us concentrate on how we treat other people. You and I are called to "do justice" in whatever our opportunities are. In the words of Christ, "Set your mind on God's kingdom and his justice before everything else, and all the rest will come to you as well." (Matthew 6:33, NEB)

The word of the Lord came to me: "*Son of man, speak to your people and say to them, If I bring the sword upon a land, and the people of the land take a man from among them, and make him their watchman; and if he sees the sword coming upon the land and blows the trumpet and warns the people; then if any one who hears the sound of the trumpet does not take warning, and the sword comes and takes him away, his blood shall be upon his own head. He heard the sound of the trumpet, and did not take warning; his blood shall be upon himself. But if he had taken warning, he would have saved his life. But if the watchman sees the sword coming and does not blow the trumpet, so that the people are not warned, and the sword comes, and takes any one of them; that man is taken away in his iniquity, but his blood I will require at the watchman's hand.*

"*So you, son of man, I have made a watchman for the house of Israel; whenever you hear a word from my mouth, you shall give them warning from me. If I say to the wicked, O wicked man, you shall surely die, and you do not speak to warn the wicked to turn from his way, that wicked man shall die in his iniquity, but his blood I will require at your hand. But if you warn the wicked to turn from his way and he does not turn from his way; he shall die in his iniquity, but you will have saved your life.*

"*And you, son of man, say to the house of Israel, Thus have you said: 'Our transgressions and our sins are upon us, and we waste away because of them; how then can we live?' Say to them, As I live, says the Lord God, I have no pleasure in the death of the wicked, but that the wicked turn from his way and live; turn back, turn back from your evil ways; for why will you die, O house of Israel?*"

Ezekiel 33:1-11

Ezekiel 33:1-11

Proper 18 (C)
Pentecost 16 (L)
Ordinary Times 23 (RC)

Why I Can't Sleep in Church

"If he had taken warning, he would have saved his life."
(v. 5)

Prayer: *You are here with us, O Lord, and we sense your presence. Speak a helpful word to us today, and give us something to take home, to think about, and to put into action. Amen*

There are many reasons why people sleep in church. Some are better reasons than others, but here are some. You be the judge. People sleep in church because:

a. They are tired after working all week.
b. They stayed up too late the night before.
c. They know more than the preacher does.
d. The pews are too comfortable.
e. It's too stuffy or warm.
f. It's boring and there's nothing else to do.
g. They trust the preacher not to say anything interesting.

There are also some good reasons why people cannot sleep in church. Here are some of those. Again, you will have to decide which reasons are better than others.

People can't sleep in church because:

a. They have insomnia. They can't even sleep at home.
b. Their morning coffee was too strong.

c. They have a child crawling all over them.
   d. They are too busy thinking of what they're going to do for a meal tonight, company on Tuesday, a test tomorrow, or a job waiting to be done.
   e. The pews are too uncomfortable.
   f. It's colder than they thought it would be.

All of these are good reasons for, and against, sleeping in church. But let me tell you one from the preacher's viewpoint.

Every pastor has heard the classic description of a preacher's job. The pastor's job is to comfort the afflicted and to afflict the comfortable. Even though that description has become somewhat hackneyed over the years, it still has a kernel of truth in it. In a broader sense, the same description fits the purpose of the church. The church is there to comfort the afflicted and to afflict the comfortable.

The first of these two functions is always the more popular and well received. Who can argue with a mission of mercy and compassion? The second function is more controversial, for certainly no one who is comfortable, likes to be disturbed or afflicted. We don't mind being disturbed if there is a true emergency, like a fire; but we don't like false alarms. Often, we're not sure if the danger is real or imagined, and we don't like to be afflicted needlessly.

The second function of the church is what we are talking about today. It is the church's responsibility to watch and warn her people of wrongdoing, false gods, dangerous tendencies and outright disobedience. If you think that sounds like a big order, it is. With all of that going on, that's why I can't sleep in church!

Ezekiel makes it clear that there are some important matters that the church, or its spokespersons need to emphasize.

1. The Need for Watching

Ezekiel told his people of the need for a watchman. I have known some men who have worked as night watchmen.

Sometimes they wear a uniform, to look more official. They carry a lot of keys. Some of them have a German Shepherd dog with them for security purposes. If anything happens, it's the watchman's job to call for help and/or do what he can. If there's anyone who needs to stay awake, it is a watchman. If a watchman falls asleep, he has committed the worst sin. His job is to watch, to warn, to be alert and to stay on the job. In the Old Testament, the watchman had a trumpet. He was the one who stood on the city wall and kept a lookout for any possible enemies. If he saw something suspicious, he was to blow the trumpet.

Near Chelan, Washington, there is a retreat center hidden away in the Cascade mountains, known as Holden Village. It was once a mining camp. In order to reach Holden, visitors must travel part of the way by boat on Lake Chelan. The rest of the trip is made via a school bus which climbs the steep mountainside by cutbacks, and then becomes a gravel road through the forest.

While visiting there last summer, we loaded the bus and piled in. Before he left the dock, the driver took a few minutes to point out that it was a dry spell, no rain had fallen for several weeks, and the forest was very dry. He stressed the restriction against smoking, and appointed two passengers to be official "fire watchers" to be on the lookout for any signs of forest fires. All passengers were urged to be on the lookout, and should report any signs of smoke to the driver immediately. He said fire is the worst enemy of those who make their home there.

The driver, a young man of 25, impressed us. He was not just reciting a memorized speech, like the airlines attendant. It sounded as though he really meant it and really cared. Without saying it directly, we knew that he loved and respected the forest far more than the casual admirer.

That lesson about watching for fires stayed with us during our stay at Holden. We were more aware of the dry forest and the dangers it could present.

Watching continues to be one of the responsibilities of God's people. It may not hold the excitement of being in the thick of the battle, but it serves a vital purpose. We may not need to watch for the Philistines or the Amalekites, but new threats have taken their place. Somebody needs to be on the lookout for injustice, discrimination, suffering and oppression. Neither can it be just one person.

Russell Hoy, author of the "Country Parson" column in the magazine *The Ohio Farmer*, told a story that emphasizes this.

"Behold a baseball team went forth to play. Just as the umpire was saying 'Batter up!' the catcher arrived and took his place. The center fielder didn't show up but sent his regrets. The third baseman didn't come because he was up late the night before. The shortstop left his glove at home. Two infielders were away on a trip, but were there in spirit. When the pitcher went to the box, he was discouraged, but he hoped for the best. He had to be pitcher, cover first, third and shortstop. When the absent players heard their team had lost, a decision was made to get a new pitcher."

2. The Need for Warning

People in the Middle West are familiar with the terms "Tornado Watch," and "Tornado Warning." The Watch, when announced on television or radio, means that the conditions are such that a tornado could occur. The Warning means that an actual tornado has been sighted in the area, and that residents should seek cover.

Besides tornadoes, life is full of warnings. Danger! Keep out! Road closed ahead! Stay back! Beware of the dog! No trespassing! Watch out! Even though many warnings sound negative, they are basically intended to protect people from harm or danger. Therefore, they have a positive intent. The warning labels on cigarettes and prescriptions, poisons and cleansers are there to protect health.

Ezekiel was called to give a warning to God's people so they might turn from their evil ways. Although his warning sounded negative, it was actually a positive sign that God loved Israel and didn't want them to perish. Jonah's mission to Nineveh was a warning to turn and repent. When they did, the city of Nineveh was spared.

When you tell your child, "Don't go out in the street," it's another way of saying, I love you and I care about you. God knows what things are harmful and dangerous for us. Life itself could be said to have a label on it that is like the one you find on a box of glassware; "Fragile: Breakable." Because of all this, it is clear that a warning needs to be heeded if it is to be effective. I think of Betty in the hospital after her operation. She pestered the doctor to let her go home before she was ready. She promised faithfully that she would not lift, or do the vacuuming or any heavy work. But Betty couldn't stand to see what needed to be done. She strained herself, and went back to the hospital, this time for twice as long as she had been before. There is a need for a warning, and a need to heed the warning.

3. The Need for the Word

God's Word to Ezekiel is an appeal to faithfulness. He says, "As I live, says the Lord God, I have no pleasure in the death of the wicked, but that the wicked turn from his way and live; turn back, turn back from your evil ways; for why will you die, O house of Israel?" (Verse 11) It is astounding to know that God cares!

It is reported that Satan once had a meeting with some of his angels to work out a strategy to win more people. He asked his associates for their counsel.

The first one said, "Let us tell the people on earth that there is no heaven. If they have nothing to hope for, they might lose interest." But Satan said, "That idea has merit, but I'm afraid the idea of heaven is too well ingrained in most peoples' minds."

The second angel offered his suggestion. "Why not tell them that there is no hell. If they have nothing to fear, we may gain some." But Satan responded, saying, "I don't think they would accept that either."

The third angel offered his advice. He said, "Why don't we keep heaven and hell, but tell the people that there is no hurry to decide between them. People can wait until the last possible moment." At that, Satan smiled and said, "That's it! That's what we'll do!" Ever since then, that plan has met with great success.

Now you know why I can't sleep in church. What is happening there is too important. I don't want to spoil your chances of sleeping in church, but I don't want you to miss this very important word from your Maker and Redeemer.

*Hear the word of the Lord, O
   people of Israel;
for the Lord has a controversy
      with the inhabitants of the
      land.
There is no faithfulness or kindness,
   and no knowledge of God in the land;
there is swearing, lying, killing,
      stealing, and committing
      adultery;
      they break all bounds and murder
      follows murder.
Therefore the land mourns,
   and all who dwell in it languish,
and also the beasts of the field,
   and the birds of the air;
   and even the fish of the sea are
      taken away.
I will return again to my place,
   until they acknowledge their
      guilt and seek my face,
   and in their distress they seek
      me, saying
      "Come, let us return to the
      Lord;
   for he has torn, that he may
      heal us;
   he has stricken, and he will
      bind us up.
After two days he will revive us;
   on the third day he will raise us
      up.
   that we may live before him.
Let us know, let us press on to
      know the Lord;
   his going forth is sure as the dawn;
he will come to us as the showers,
   as the spring rains that water
      the earth."*

*What shall I do with you, O
   Ephraim?
What shall I do with you, O
   Judah?
Your life is like a morning cloud,
   like the dew that goes early
      away.
Therefore I have hewn them by
   the prophets,
   I have slain them by the words
      of my mouth,
   and my judgment goes forth as
      the light.
For I desire steadfast love and not
   sacrifice,
   the knowledge of God, rather
      then burnt offerings.*

Hosea 4:1-3, 5-15—6:6

Hosea 4:1-3; 5:15—6:6

Proper 19 (C)
Pentecost 17 (L)
Ordinary Time 24 (RC)

Honest to Goodness Religion

"For I desire steadfast love and not sacrifice." (v. 6)

Prayer: *Lord, Instill in us a sense of wonder that you really care what we do with our lives. Lead us to a greater appreciation of your love so we may never take it for granted. Amen*

There is a captivating story written by an English novelist, C. E. Montague, entitled *Rough Justice*.[9] The story tells of a little boy, Bron, who was brought to church for the first time in his life, where his uncle was the vicar. For the boy it was an intriguing experience. He was impressed with the atmosphere, the choir and the sound of the organ. His uncle stepped into the pulpit and began to preach.

The boy listened intently. The pastor told a strange story, of a man who was the holiest, most kind and wonderful man who ever lived. Sick people sought him out and were made well. People with great sadness were made happy again. Some whose lives had been all wrong were forgiven and taught how to forgive others. People afraid of dying were promised they could live forever. This wonderful person, Jesus, touched and changed many lives.

But not everyone approved of him. Some hated him and wanted to get rid of him. They arrested him, put him on trial, took him with two criminals and killed him on a cruel

---

9. A. Reuben Gornitzka, *Seriously, Now*, Augsburg Publishing House, Minneapolis, Minnesota, 1956, pp. 71-72.

thing called a "cross." The uncle went on to say that this man was not dead but lived again, and now he was looking for people to go out and do for the world what he had done.

As the service ended, worshippers left their pews and went out the aisles. Bron's nurse left with the others, but when she got outside she realized that the boy was not with her. Bron was thoroughly moved by the story of this Man and could not understand why people around him were so calm about this remarkable happening. They walked out of the church as though nothing unusual had been told to them. Bron was still in the pew, sobbing. His nurse found him and said, "Bron, you mustn't take it so much to heart; people might think you are queer."

It may be that we are among those who hear the greatest news in the world, and walk out serenely, with no more emotion than if we had just paid the electric bill. It may be that we do not take that remarkable message to heart any more. We have become used to it and hardly think about it. We have learned not to take it too seriously, for people might think us queer.

The Lord is not pleased with people who simply go through the motions of worship, who leave their faith and their Christianity in the pew with the hymnbook. Hosea encourages us, if we are to discover what "Honest to goodness" religion is all about, to:

- Face the Problem,
- Find the Answer,
- Follow the Real Thing.

1. Face the Problem (Hosea 4:1-3)

The Lord has a charge to bring against the people who live in the land. The problem is that there is no faithfulness, no kindness, and no knowledge of God in the land. What a sweeping indictment! God's people have become the

"Un-Generation." They are:

Unfaithful	Unloving	Unfit	Unrighteous	Unworthy
Unkind	Uncaring	Unfair	Unforgiving	Unlawful
Unknowing	Unconcerned	Unholy	Unscrupulous	Unpleasant

As the Lord looks around at his people he sees moral chaos and degenerate behavior. There is a flagrant disregard for God's law, the Ten Commandments.

God's people are characterized like the crowd that gathered in the busy section of a large city. High up on a narrow ledge of a hotel building, a young man was threatening to jump. As the news traveled, more spectators came to watch. Some boys shouted, "Jump! Jump!" A woman yelled, "What's the matter? Are you chicken?" One man offered to bet ten dollars that the youth would jump.

Several attempts were made to coax the young man back. He refused. Finally, several hours later, his seven-year-old nephew pleaded successfully with him to step back into the building to safety.

As the crowd began to disperse, a woman said, "He made me miss my favorite TV program." The man who lost his bet went off grumbling.

It is a commentary on our times when we witness tragedy without compassion. God has shown mercy to us that we may learn how to show mercy to others. Sometimes, however, as Hosea observes, the quality of mercy is sadly lacking.

The problem, as Hosea points out, goes even beyond moral behavior. He implies that there is some relationship between the way people treat each other and the way they treat their environment. Animals, birds, fish all suffer because of human greed and exploitations. The land and the sea bear the brunt of our technological capacity to consume, pollute and poison the environment.

An exhibit in the Cleveland Museum of Natural History caught the eye of many visitors. In the Mammal section there was a large mirror with the inscription: Homo Sapiens.

The most numerous large mammal on earth, a dangerous animal whose misuse of world resources and uncontrolled population growth is a threat to all living things.

For us who are classified as homo sapiens, it's not very flattering, but it is true.

There is a problem. It involves how people treat each other, and how they treat the world.

2. *Find the Answer* (Hosea 5:15—6:3)

According to Hosea, the Lord, seeing the disastrous behavior of his children, has had enough. He returns to his place, knowing that sooner or later these children will want to come and seek him. When they wake up and come to their senses, they will start to look for a solution.

It is said that the Lord and the Archangel Michael were conversing in the Communications Room of heaven. In a loud continuous torrent, all prayers of humankind were ascending from the earth. It was a babel of sound. Some prayers were passionate, others were registering complaints, some were urgent requests and others were questions.

Somewhat overwhelmed, Michael said to the Lord, "I beg your pardon, Sir, but sometimes I think it might have been a mistake to let people learn to talk. It is difficult to understand them with so much speaking." But the Lord said, "I don't listen to the words as much as I do to their lives." He closed the window, and the noise of the tempest of words ceased. The Lord pressed a button on the receiver, and over the speaker came just one prayer. It was a condensed version of a great number of prayers that came up from the lives of people. A quavering voice was heard, "O Lord, if it does not cost too much, we would like to be faithful, courageous, loving and forgiving."

"If it does not cost too much . . ." How true. For many of us, religion is conditional. People are always on the lookout for bargain-sale salvation, cheap commitment and discount discipleship. We have a wistful yearning to do better and to make some real changes in our lives, but fortunately (usually) the impulse does not last too long and we return to normal.

God's people instinctively know where to go for help and where to find answers. Even though the Lord has allowed them to feel the results of their rebellion, they know they can come back. They say, "Let us return to the Lord."

The implication of these first few verses of Hosea 6 is that God will indeed welcome his wayward children, no matter what they have done. One has the feeling, "We can always go home . . . he'll never turn us away." It's an attitude of easy complacency: everything will be okay in a couple days.

This is the shallowness of popular religion. There is no sense of awe, no sense of wonder, no sense of guilt. There is nothing but the carefree assumption that God is ready at any time to welcome those who return to him with open arms. God is as dependable as each day's sunrise and as the spring rains. It is true that God welcomes the sinner, but somehow it seems wrong for us to presume on that privilege and to take it for granted.

3. *Follow the Real Thing* (Hosea 6:4-6)

It is no wonder that the Lord is exasperated with his people. He speaks to them: "What am I going to do with you? You come to me only when you want something from me. You come to me only when there is no place else to go and you need help. Your 'love' is like the morning haze, or the dew in the front yard. It's there for a short time, then it is gone. I have sent prophets to urge you to change your ways, but it hasn't seemed to have helped. What am I to do with you?"

The Lord wants something other than routine sacrifice. He doesn't want empty ritual. As the *Living Bible* says it, "I don't want your sacrifices — I want your love."

We had a chance to see real, practical love in action during a recent trip to Washington, D.C. My wife and I had a chance to assist on McKenna's Wagon, a "meals on wheels" for the homeless poor of the city. The "Wagon" was an old van, operating out of Martha's Table, a food distribution center.

We loaded the van with trays of sandwiches made of lunch meat, cheese or peanut butter; a few bags of apples; containers of coffee and tea; and a large steaming kettle of hearty soup. As we made our way through the late-afternoon rush hour, we tried to keep the kettle from sliding around too much on the sharp turns. Since it was raining, we also tried to avoid the holes in the van's roof. At the small public park where food was to be dispensed, a line had already formed. It took only a few minutes to open the side window and begin to hand out soup, sandwiches and hot drinks.

Two young men were with us on the van, who regularly donated a few hours on the Wagon after their working day. "Red" was a waiter at a fashionable restaurant, and Giles was in computer sales. I can still see the driver, Giles, the salesman in his three-piece suit, standing in the rain, pouring hot coffee and tea into cups for homeless and hungry men.

While driving bumper-to-bumper in the streets of Washington, Giles shared his philosophy about the Wagon with us. When we asked him, "What if we run out of food?" he answered, "We never run out. It's like the story where a lot of people were fed and they gathered up sixty baskets afterwards. There's always enough."

When we commented about the heavy traffic, Giles said, "There are angels traveling with this van. You can't see them, but they are here. They watch over this mission."

Many beautiful things can be said about love. But when it comes right down to it, honest-to-goodness love is more often a peanut butter sandwich than it is a noble feeling of pity. Love acts. Love does. Love serves. Love cares. Love is practical. The Lord has a great challenge for us. His challenge is to follow the real thing, and not to worry whether others may consider us queer. You won't need to worry whether your religion is honest-to-goodness.

When Israel was a child, I
  loved him,
and out of Egypt I called my
  son.
The more I called them,
  the more they went from me;
they kept sacrificing to the Baals,
  and kept burning incense to idols.
Yet it was I who taught Ephraim
  to walk,
  I took them up in my arms;
  but they did not know that I
    healed them.
I led them with cords of compassion,
  with the bands of love,
and I became to them as one
  who eases the yoke on their
    jaws,
  and I bent down to them and
    fed them.
They shall return to the land of
  Egypt.
  and Assyria shall be their king,
  because they have refused to
    return to me.
The sword shall rage against their
    cities,
  consume the bars of their gates,
  and devour them in their fortresses.
My people are bent on turning
    away from me;
  so they are appointed to the
    yoke,
  and none shall remove it.
How can I give you up, O
    Ephraim!
  How can I hand you over, O
    Israel!
How can I make you like Admah!
  How can I treat you like Zeboiim!

My heart recoils within me,
  my compassion grows warm
    and tender.
I will not execute my fierce anger,
  I will not again destroy
    Ephraim;
For I am God and not man,
  the Holy One in your midst,
  and I will not come to destroy.
They shall go after the Lord,
  he will roar like a lion;
yea, he will roar,
  and his sons shall come trembling
    from the west;
they shall come trembling like
    birds from Egypt,
  and like doves from the land of
    Assyria;
  and I will return them to their
    homes, says the Lord.

Hosea 11:1-11

Hosea 11:1-11

Proper 20 (C)
Pentecost 18 (L)
Ordinary Time 25 (RC)

The God Who Doesn't Give Up

"How can I give you up, O Ephraim!" (v. 8)

Prayer: *Dear Father, we cannot fool you or pretend to be something we're not; you know us too well. Open our minds and our understanding to know you as best we can, and to grow in appreciation of your great mercy. Amen*

"I've given him a chance three times now. Three times he let me down. I'm not going to be generous any more. I've had it. I don't want to get burned again."

This was Douglas, a man usually willing to go the second mile. He was known for his good nature and his willingness to give a person a chance. In this case, however, he had gone far enough.

Douglas was a carpenter who had a small construction business. Against his better judgment, he hired a man called Sandy to work for him. Sandy was a good worker, but not always dependable. When Doug was depending on him for a Monday morning roof job, Sandy never showed up. He had had too much of a weekend. After a reprimand, Doug gave him another chance. But it happened again, and then a third time. It was then that Doug said to Sandy, "I've given you three chances now. That's enough. I'm through giving any more chances. I'm sorry, but I'm going to have to let you go."

You may know of someone like that. You may even have experienced some version of this yourself. When someone takes advantage of you, you may be willing to forgive them once, twice, or even three times; but there usually comes a point where you say, "That's enough. I don't want to go through this again." The feeling is one of exasperation, disappointment and anger. You have bent over backwards to give a person a chance, but that person has failed to do his or her part.

Some of the same feeling of exasperation can be seen in Hosea 11. Instead of a contractor and an undependable worker, however, here it is rather the picture of a father, and a son who is undependable. This son chooses to disregard everything his father has taught him. In fact, this son seems bent on his own destruction and there's nothing that the father or anyone else can do. Listen to this lament:

> *When Israel was a child, I loved him, and out of Egypt I called my son. (v. 1)*
>
> *The more I called them, the more they went from me; they kept sacrificing to the Baals, and burning incense to idols. (v. 2)*

Parenting is a powerful image in the Scriptures. We should pause to point out, however, that even though Hosea portrays a father and a son, God's love described here is parental rather than paternal. This is a text which can be thought of equally well in either maternal or paternal terms. The acts of nurturing pictured in the first few verses are appropriate to both mothers and fathers. Commentator James Ward says, "The parental metaphor which is the underlying image of Hosea 11 transcends the masculine-feminine dichotomy and is therefore one of the most adequate symbols of God in the Bible."[10] If that doesn't make sense, we can put it in other words. God is both father and mother and cares for us with the best qualities that a mother or father combined, can give.

---

10. James M. Ward, *Amos-Hosea*, Knox Preaching Guides, John Hayes, ed., John Knox Press, 1981, p. 87.

Being a parent can be an enjoyable experience. Do you remember bringing your first child home from the hospital, and how the atmosphere of your home was changed? There was a smell of baby powder in the air, and the house was hushed when baby was taking a nap.

Your child grasped your fingers tightly in taking those first hesitant steps, laughing and giggling;

You lifted your child up in your arms with love;

You gave your child hugs and kisses which were returned to you;

You placed your child in the high chair for a meal which inevitably was made a mess;

You bought your child toys and shoes and clothes;

You did everything you could to give your child a good upbringing.

Being a parent is a demanding pastime. Hosea indicates that like any other parent, God has watched over his own as they were growing up. Children aren't really aware of the sacrifices their parents make, so that the kids can have new shoes, play in the little league or take piano lessons. Children have no way of knowing how concerned their parents are about a balanced diet, their child's education, or what they are watching on television. Children consider it a bother when their parents insist on knowing where their children are going, with whom, and for how long. Parents carry out the thankless tasks of arranging dental checkups and making sure there's enough milk in the house. Parents are the people who require thank-you notes to be written, and a bank account started. One mother said, "When my children were born, I just figured that I was making a pretty strong commitment to each of them for at least the first eighteen years of their lives."

What a disappointment it is, then, when parents find out that their best intentions and their best efforts seem to have meant nothing. The child has rebelled and run off. The Lord speaks through Hosea in verse 7, "My people are bent on turning away from me." William Beck, in his translation of the

Bible, puts it this way: "My people are hopelessly determined to desert me." It reminds me of what one baseball manager said about the attendance at baseball games: "If the people don't want to come, there's nothing that's going to stop them!"

The Lord also laments what his children are doing. Many parents can identify with that. You try to reach out to your child, and your child runs from you. What is a parent to do when their children choose to ignore or reject any advice given them? What is a parent to do when their children associate with a group of friends of whom the parents don't approve? One can imagine the heartache and the chagrin of the parents of the prodigal son when they heard of his plans to leave home.

Being a parent, then, is also risky business. The risk is always there that they might just reject your love and everything you've given them. A man in the hospital was deeply disappointed because his children, mostly grown up and married, did not come to see him. He said, "I've given them everything, and what do I get in return? Nothing . . . and it hurts."

According to Hosea, the Lord seems to give up on his children, saying that they shall return to the land of Egypt and Assyria shall be their king. If that's what they want, let them reap the results of their disobedience. They will feel the harsh facts of life, when enemies with swords come upon them, breaking through their city gates. The *Good News Bible* says, "War will sweep through their cities and break down the city gates. It will destroy my people because they do what they themselves think best. They insist on turning away from me."

Although it sounds like the Lord is giving up on his people, he is simply stating what is going to happen. Likewise, parents can see what is happening in their child's life. They know where it's likely to end up, and they know the child is headed for grief and trouble. God is not sending the punishment, but knows that it will happen as a result of their rejection of his way.

So the Lord admits that he cannot give up on his children. He asks, rhetorically, "How can I give you up, O Ephraim?

How can I hand you over, O Israel?" (Hosea 11:8) Can the Lord just scratch them out of his book? Can he consider them like Admah and Zeboiim, cities that were conflagrated with fire along with Sodom and Gomorrah? (Deuteronomy 29:23) Some parents go so far as to disown their children. They make it clear that the child is not welcome any more. The Lord speaks as a parent, whose heart says, "These are still my children, no matter what. I cannot disown them."

I remember reading of a woman who had twin boys, but who had entirely different personalities. One was the kind of a boy who enjoyed Scouts, had a paper route, did well in school, and was elected to lead the student council in high school. He went to college and studied law. The other son was a boy who was rebellious, always getting into trouble, and being called into the principal's office. He quit school, was picked up by the police several times, and was finally arrested on a felony charge.

By a strange coincidence, the day one of her sons was to receive his degree was the same day the other son was to receive his sentence for his crime. The mother went to the graduation ceremony, but while she was there, proud of the accomplishments of one of her sons, her heart was in another place, in a courtroom, grieving for the son who couldn't stay out of trouble.

Does a mother forget her son because of what he has done? Does the Lord give up on his children because of what they have done? The answer, clearly, is no. The Lord says, "My heart recoils at such a thing!" His compassion grows warm and tender. The first line of one of Frederick Faber's hymns describes God's nature in these words, "There's a wideness in God's mercy, like the wideness of the sea."

The Lord explains why he is the way he is. "For I am God and not man." (Hosea 11:9) What a significant pronouncement that is! If I were "man" I would act differently! If I were man I would take revenge, and return hate for hate. I would teach those smart kids a lesson they'd never forget.

But the Lord is God and not man. "My thoughts are not your thoughts, neither are your ways my ways, says the Lord." (Isaiah 55:8) "As a father pities his children, so the Lord pities those who fear him." (Psalm 103:13) God does things in ways that people would never dream of doing them. He says, "I am the Holy One in your midst, and I will not come to destroy."

There's a story passed on by Gerald Wilkinson, that Native American people in the Southwest tell their children. It reflects the merciful attribute of God. It involves an old man who was reputed to be the wisest man in the village. One day some children decided to test him. They caught a little bird and decided they would go to him with the little bird behind their back and ask him if what they had in their hand was alive or dead. If he said it was alive, they would crush the bird. If he said it was dead, they would let it fly away.

So they went to him holding the bird behind their back. They said, "Old man, is what we have behind our back alive or dead?" The old man looked at them and said, "The answer to that question, my children, is in your hands."

He equated the bird to the earth and advised, "You have become a powerful people and you have caught a little bird and hold it in your hands. I hope that you will find the wisdom to let it fly away."

God is a parent who treats us mercifully. He also wants us to find the wisdom to treat others with compassion.

The Lord does not give up easily. He looks forward to the day when his children will return, responding to his call. What a great day that will be! They will come from all over. They will come back to where they belong. Like the swallows to Capistrano, they will come back.

The picture of "coming home," described in the last verses of this text, is an experience filled with emotion. You hear things like: "It feels so good to be home," "We've missed you," "It's so good to see you!"

The God who doesn't give up is always looking ahead to that reunion. He wants you and me back where we belong — within his Kingdom.

www.ingramcontent.com/pod-product-compliance
Lightning Source LLC
Chambersburg PA
CBHW060850050426
42453CB00008B/926